LOST BOUNDARIES

LOST

BOUNDARIES

———

W. L. WHITE

New York

HARCOURT, BRACE AND COMPANY

LOST BOUNDARIES

I

The Secret

BEFORE you learn what Albert Johnston, Jr., was told at the age of sixteen and why he was not told it before, you should know something of his background. It would be dull but accurate to say that, until he was told, we are dealing with a normal New England boy. He was born in Boston in 1925 while his father was still a medical student at the University of Chicago. When Albert was four, his first memories begin in the little town of Gorham, New Hampshire, where his father was now the leading country doctor serving its 2,500 people, who live at the foot of Mount Washington to which vacationists swarm for winter skiing and summer coolness, with special trains in the fall when the maple leaves turn red and gold.

Here Albert played over the hills, learned to ski, camped out on long Boy Scout hikes, climbed Mount Washington to look down on the other rolling New England hills, made the high-school honor roll, was

elected president of his high-school class, and took
piano lessons. Looking back on it you would agree
that, before he was told, he had the healthy background of rural New England—a normal American
boy and Yankee both in his outlook and in his flat
accent.

This was also true of his heredity, which had been
for many generations a mingling of the old American
blood stocks, with the possible exception of a great-
grandfather who had come from Germany and who,
according to Albert's mother, accounted for the fact
that little Albert was darker than most of his high-
school classmates, with brown eyes, a high, prominent nose and dark, curly hair.

When Albert was fifteen the family left Gorham,
where his father had been a Mason, a Rotarian, park
commissioner, and chairman of the school board, to
move down to Keene, bigger than Gorham but much
like it, another typical New England town with its
two-hundred-year-old Congregational Church on the
main square, its white spire high above the green
elm leaves. Albert, like most children in rural New
England, had been going to Congregational Sunday
School since he could first remember. His father,
who had taken a year off to study Roentgenology
(of course at Harvard) was now working in Keene's

leading hospital and Albert, who was planning on Dartmouth, was preparing at nearby Mount Hermon school.

It was a tolerant, cosmopolitan place, and here this little New England boy got his outlook broadened, for one of his schoolmates was a Negro, Charles Duncan.

Negroes in rural New Hampshire are a curiosity. Once a Negro tramp had been given a night's lodging in the Gorham jail, and next morning Albert, with all the other youngsters, had gone down to peer through the bars "to see the black man." Occasionally a summer visitor brought along a Negro cook. Albert had never seen any reason to question the prevailing opinion that Negroes were inferior, stupid, ignorant, and lazy, that they swept floors or were housemaids or at best played pianos. He had heard of the Negro scientist George Washington Carver, but he was the exception that proved the rule. Of course his parents, like most tolerant New Englanders, had taught him that it was impolite to use the word "nigger," and that they should be referred to as "colored people."

So Charlie Duncan, who was the son of Todd Duncan who sang in *Porgy and Bess,* and who was later to become a leader of his Dartmouth class, was

a surprise to Albert. Charlie was quiet, well man-
nered, popular in Mount Hermon, and brilliant in
his studies, winning not only the history prize but
several others to become salutatorian of his class.
He was also on the ski team, and a year ahead of
Albert, who, toward the end of his junior year, was
elected captain for the next.

But at this point there was a little incident. The
Mount Hermon team was to be represented at the
big meet at Meriden, but the coach ruled that only
six could go, and did not include captain-elect Albert
Johnston in the group.

Whereupon Charlie Duncan, who was scheduled
to go, said to the team, "I think Peanut [Albert's
school nickname] is a better skier than I am," and
told the boys he would like to give up his place so
Albert could go. In the end the coach relented and
promised seven could go, so when Albert went home
for the weekend he was still bubbling over this
schoolboy's victory.

This home is one of the most beautiful in Keene.
It sits on a large corner lot of one of Keene's finest
residential streets, shaded by the ancient elms of
New England, and why should it not also have been
one of the most secure? Had not Dr. Johnston solidly established himself in New Hampshire? Was

he not steadily moving up in his profession? What could be more stable?

But on this particular weekend there was trouble, as the boy could sense. Something about the Navy. His father, who had seen the war coming, had early answered the Navy's call for volunteers. After some time, he had been notified that he was accepted, and that a commission as lieutenant commander would presently come through.

Now there seemed to be some hitch. The Navy seemed to be out. Dad was all lathered up about it, talking a lot with Mom. Neither had told him what it was about. Dad had already had a couple of drinks.

Albert couldn't see that it mattered much. Of course Dad was probably all set on one of those nice blue uniforms and all that braid. But what difference did it make if the Navy had decided Dad was too old, or too fat, or something like that? After all, most men of his age weren't anxious to leave a good practice. Many were figuring all the angles as to how they could stay out. Anyway, maybe they would take Dad later.

Albert couldn't see that it mattered, and decided he would take a bath and then call a couple of girls to see how things were for a date tonight. Certainly it didn't matter as much as the news that he was, after all, going with the ski team.

He was to use the tub in the room which adjoined his parents' bedroom and, as he turned on the hot water, he began telling them the whole story of that ski incident, of Charlie Duncan's offer to give up his place so Al could go, how popular Charlie was and what a good athlete, how he led his whole class in studies, and how everyone liked Charlie, even if he *was* colored.

Although it happened several years ago, Albert still remembers as though it were only last night. He remembers how, as he praised Charlie Duncan, his father "beamed all up." And then said to Mom:

"I'm going to tell that boy."

And how his mother almost screamed from the bedroom:

"No! No! Don't do it! Don't ever do it!"

"I've got to do it," his father answered. Then Dad stepped back into the bedroom and when, half a minute later, he returned to the bathroom door, he had a third drink in his hand.

"Turn off the water," he said, and Albert did.

"Do you know something, boy?" he asked.

"No, what?" said Albert.

"Well, you're colored."

Albert still remembers the funny sensation that went through him, and for a minute he didn't say anything. Then he said, "Well, how come?"

"I'm colored and your mother's colored."

Albert had his shirt off, but he did not continue dressing for the date, because he knew he would not want to call either of those girls tonight. He walked slowly into his parents' bedroom.

There his father explained that his own mother was colored, and also his father, although he didn't look it.

"How about Mom, is she colored too?" asked Albert, even though this had already been answered.

They explained that both Grandma and Grandpa on Mom's side were colored, although they didn't look it; in fact, all four grandparents were colored, but all could get by.

Albert didn't feel anything but dazed, he remembers.

Then they said he must not tell anyone of this, because of what it might do to Dad, and that the two younger children hadn't been told yet. They explained what "passing" was, and how Dad had had to do it, not because he was ashamed of being colored, but only to make their living.

Then his mother asked him, now that he knew, how he felt about it?

Albert said he felt proud of it, and that he hoped to do something for the Negro.

This greatly pleased his father, and he jumped up and shook Albert's hand, even though Albert was only sixteen. It was the first time this had ever happened in exactly this way, and of course it pleased Albert. But he kept feeling more and more dazed.

Now his father and mother, both excited, began telling him the whole story of how it had happened, the story of both their lives tumbling out at once, each so excited they kept interrupting each other to add details. But we can start with the story of Albert's mother, as he finally learned it that night in the bedroom of the beautiful old house on the oldest and best residential street of Keene, New Hampshire, within sight of the two-hundred-year-old white spire of the Congregational Church which Albert attended, a spire pointed like a white arrow up through the stately old elms, toward the black sky and shimmering stars.

II

Passing

ALBERT'S mother had been christened Thyra Agatha in the Catholic church in New Orleans, in 1903, where she had lived until she was nine. Her grandfather had been shipping commissioner of the Port of New Orleans. He had originally come from Germany, and in New Orleans had married a colored woman. Thyra's father was working as a clerk in the post office. At that time there was segregation everywhere in New Orleans except in the federal offices.

But when the Democrats elected Woodrow Wilson in 1912, her father, fearing more segregation and wanting to avoid embarrassment, applied for a transfer to the Boston post office. The children had been enrolled in the colored public schools of New Orleans, but they had had many disagreeable experiences there because they were so fair, which the white teachers resented.

Dad came ahead to Boston and leased a duplex

in Roxbury for his family, and also for two little
cousins who came with them and who were a little
darker. When the people in the other side of the
duplex saw the two cousins they threatened to
move. But after the children started to school and
they got to know them better, there was no more
trouble. The Johnstons say it is usually that way.

The Baumann children went through grade school
and high school the only Negroes in their class, and
mixing with everyone. The family also had Negro
friends, but they kept these separate from the others.
They included Negro lawyers, doctors, and dentists
living in Boston, professional men whose practice
was usually confined to Boston's small Negro col-
ony.

In appearance Thyra Baumann had a creamy,
soft skin, wavy, light brown hair, and blue eyes. In
high school she had taken the commercial course,
so after she graduated she went to work as a stenog-
rapher for the Mellins Food Company. On her
application blank she put down "white" in order
to get the job. Her mother had told all the children
not to put down anything on such blanks—"let them
fill it out."

In her next job application they didn't want any
Catholics, so on her application she lied, wrote

"Protestant," and got it. They assumed she was white and she let them think so. She didn't mix much with them. And also, "Daddy was skeptical about me going out with dark men. He was afraid I would be seen with them and lose my job if it were known I was colored."

So her father was very much disturbed when Joe Carter, the dark Negro halfback of Brown University, invited her to go with a group to the Brown-Harvard game, and to the party later, as his date. Dad forbade her to go to the game with this colored group where she might be seen and recognized, so she told Joe she had to work during the game. Afterward she went with him to the formal party in a taxi. There was little chance that she would be recognized in the cab.

"My Dad was very fair and handsome," says Thyra. "He said he had brought us up from New Orleans to get us out of it. I liked Joe very much, but my parents felt that if I married a dark man, I would be 'going back.' So Dad and Mom would take Joe's letters out of my mail, and I couldn't understand why I didn't hear from him." And that was soon over.

Her vacation in 1923 came in September, and she decided to take a two-week trip to Chicago, to visit colored friends who had a daughter her age, Marcella Walker. There are small colored groups all over the country who form a closely knit social class, the Johnstons say, and they pass you on from one town to another. Long before she arrived, her Chicago girl friend had her dated up solidly for her entire stay with the most eligible young Chicago colored professional men, but the one she liked best, and broke several of her other dates for, was Albert C. Johnston, then a pre-medical student at the University of Chicago. He was a little darker than she, yet not so dark that he had any trouble buying orchestra seats to see the Dolly sisters who were playing in *Topsy and Eva*, although Chicago theaters were quite biased against colored people.

The day before she left he took her out to the University to show her its grounds and his colored fraternity house, Kappa Alpha Psi, and asked her why didn't she stay, and marry him. She had even gone down to an agency and had the promise of a job when her mother telegraphed and then telephoned from Boston that she was to come home at once. Her parents were worried. They did not know whether Albert Johnston was light or dark, or in or out of the social set.

So she returned, and then it was Albert Johnston

who wrote, telegraphed, phoned, and finally came that Christmas to Boston where they were married. Her mother and Dad at first had not approved. After she had fallen in love with him, what they really wanted to know was, what did this man look like?

Albert Johnston, Sr., had been born in Chicago on August 17, 1900, and had been registered as a Negro. His father had come from Michigan where he had been raised on a farm. This father was even lighter than the son, and on the father's side, as far back as the family can be traced, all had lived in the North and none were ever slaves. But his mother had come from the South and both her parents had been Mississippi slaves.

Johnston's father, who was agent for a Chicago real estate company and had to pass as white to hold this job, did not encourage colored people to visit the house.

"On the other hand," Johnston says, "my mother is equally prejudiced against whites. The blacker they are, the better she likes them. My brothers carry out my mother's prejudices—I have neither. I have never held it against blacks or browns or whites."

When Albert Johnston entered Chicago public

schools there was no segregation and only a few
thousand Negroes in Chicago. When he was twelve,
people began asking what he was, and since he was
embarrassed to say he was part Negro, he told them
he was one-eighth Cherokee Indian, which he is.
He attended a colored church until he was eight,
and after that a white Presbyterian church. In Wen-
dell Phillips High School all of his friends, including
girls, were white, and he remembers only one Negro
in his graduating class.

His mother said she would rather see him dead
than married to a white girl. "At first," he says, "I
found colored girls distasteful, but presently found
my own race more interesting than the white.

"As a colored student at the University of Chicago,
I wasn't invited or expected to attend social func-
tions. But no one seemed to mind this social ex-
clusion. We had our own fraternity house, our own
life, and there was considerable talent in this small
group." Rush Medical College then had a quota of
two Negroes per class of whom he was one, and the
other was Ralph Scull, who was for years the only
colored teacher at Rush. The two were paired together in laboratory work. "I was well treated by
both the students and the faculty," Johnston re-

members. "No one is prejudiced against you if they know you."

Ordinarily undergraduates at Rush were required to serve as junior internes at nearby Presbyterian Hospital, but Johnston and the other colored student were told that it would not be necessary for them to take this required course. The real reason was that Presbyterian feared its white patients would object. Remembering this, Dr. Johnston now smiles. "I have since practiced medicine for eighteen years," he says, "and have never had a colored patient."

After his marriage in 1924 to Thyra, medical school was a struggle. Part of the time they lived together, but after little Albert, Jr., was born she lived in Boston while the young father struggled to support himself, pay his tuition, and send something to his family, by working as a porter and dining-car waiter on a dozen railroads during vacations, and at nights in the post office and at various odd jobs while he attended medical school.

But upon graduation, before he could get his M.D. degree from Rush Medical College it was necessary for him to interne at some first-rate hospital which Rush approved. Only four Negro hospitals, in Washington, D. C., Chicago, St. Louis, and Kansas City, were open to Negro internes, and these

were then not up to the standard of hospitals ordinarily acceptable to Rush.

So Johnston wrote to what he thought were the
most liberal hospitals in the country, hoping they
would take him in.

Toledo seemed most anxious to have him until, on
personal interview, they found he was colored. They
then explained it was not their policy. Worcester
(Massachusetts) City Hospital didn't exactly say
this (he had made great sacrifice to get money for
the trip) but Johnston is sure that if he had been
white he could have got in.

Then suddenly he got a welcoming telegram from
Maine General Hospital at Portland, which had just
concluded a not too successful experiment with all-
women internes. He started out in great fear that
here again they might recognize and reject him.

But they didn't ask, so why should he end his
chances by telling them? Had he gone to Howard
or Meharry Medical Schools, which are exclusively
Negro, of course they would have known. But a
diploma from Rush proves nothing of its bearer's
racial background—proves only that he has the brains
to finish one of the nation's stiffest and best medical
schools.

In Boston his young wife Thyra had found in a

pawnshop a $25 suit of clothes that fitted him well, so he could make a good appearance. Out of the other money she saved from her job, she bought him shirts, underwear, and even some neckties. In Maine they banqueted him at the Portland Club and he was accepted. His pay would be only his board and room, but every weekend he would be free to visit his family in Boston.

Dr. Johnston, looking back on it, says that he was very lucky at Maine General. He made few mistakes, was well liked, and got along fine "as soon as I got over my fear that my racial identity would be recognized." After that he danced and played tennis with everyone as the other internes did.

Later they told him, "You know when you first came, some of us thought you were a Filipino, or maybe a Hawaiian or a Jew—we didn't know what you were." And Dr. Johnston smiled along with them. So long as they didn't care enough to ask directly, why should he tell?

There were few Negroes in Portland but finally one came to the hospital as a patient—she was a cook for one of the trustees. And Dr. Johnston remembers that, as an interne, he overdid himself giving her good service. So he was surprised when the head doctor called him, said he had had a complaint from the woman, and warned him sternly that he was in New England now, that Yankees didn't share the race prejudices of Chicagoans and other Midwesterners. The woman, Dr. Johnston points out, was looking for prejudice even where there was none, as people often do.

When he finished his interneship, this hospital chief called him in to offer him a job as pathologist. But at the same time there came another chance. The head of the board of registration, Dr. Adam Leighton, told him that an old friend of his, Dr. H. H. Bryant, had recently died in the village of Gorham in northern New Hampshire at the foot of Mount Washington, where he had been general practitioner for many years, leaving a fine practice and an excellent opening for a young doctor who didn't mind doing everything at all hours of the day and night.

Young Dr. Johnston found it even better than he expected. Dr. Bryant's widow would sell his office equipment and good will for $1,000, and also would rent the new doctor her husband's office and look after his telephone calls.

To finance this, he found he could borrow $2,000 at the Gorham bank on the strength of the good impression he made, and he immediately stepped into a busy country practice. He wired his wife telling her of these wonders, of the beautiful scenery, and of the five-room furnished apartment which could be rented.

But it was a practice which required some understanding and Dr. Johnston will never forget his first case. That day he had driven 350 miles on a winding White Mountain road through a sleetstorm, with his head hanging around the side of the windshield (the car had no defroster) and had gone to bed exhausted. At three in the morning the doorbell rang. A gnarled old Yankee gave him an unfamiliar street address. He was to come at once.

The doctor walked a block to get his car and then spent half an hour starting it at 32 below zero. When he finally got to the address, he found it closer to his warm bedroom than his car had been. In the parlor sat the same gnarled old Yankee farmer.

"Who's sick?"

The old man took his pipe out of his mouth. "I am."

"What's the matter?"

"Piles."

"How long you had 'em?"

"Eighteen years."

"Any worse now than they have been?"

"Nope."

The New Hampshire Yankee simply wanted to know if their new doctor was lazy, or if he really would come when called. After that he was called constantly—to deliver babies, to treat every known disease of childhood and old age, to set a dog's broken leg and to pull innumerable teeth, although he had had no dentistry. He was paid not only in cash but in butter, eggs, and every known form of farm produce. The people were honest. A few obviously could not pay at all. These were treated by the new doctor as he treated the rest, but they never got a bill. Because, why bother? But presently from those who could pay and promptly on the first of the month, the money was rolling in.

It was a substantial little country practice and clearly they liked the new doctor as much as he liked them. Now he felt secure enough to send for his wife.

He met her at the station. As they passed the grocery store on the way home she asked timidly, "Is there any food in the house? Do you think we can spend $5 for groceries?" Proudly the doctor pulled from his pocket a green fistful of collections.

"Hell," he said, "you can buy the place!"

If you couldn't quite buy it you could make it like

you, and soon people began to call on the new doctor's wife. First the lady upstairs showed her how to light the coal stove. The doctor had laid in plenty of coal, but it was all big furnace chunks. The lady explained she should not only have a smaller size, but also needed kindling and under that old newspapers to start the fire, matters which were mysteries to the city girl and her city husband.

Hardly had she solved them when the others began to call. Some came with Mrs. Bryant, the wife of the old doctor; soon all the women in town had called. And also the Congregational minister, who asked if he might enroll the children in the cradle class. He didn't ask their religion any more than he asked their color, so the doctor and his wife said, why not? Neither had given much thought to religion; this seemed to be the church to which almost everybody belonged, and why shouldn't their children grow up with the others?

As for prejudice in the town there was quite a little, but it all seemed to be friction between the old Yankee stock and the French Catholics who were coming down from Canada. And the Ku Klux Klan was organizing. Presumably they were also against the Jews, but even the Gorham Klan didn't apply this to old Abe Stahl who lived on Main

Street, the only Jew in Gorham. Jews might be bad, but old Abe was all right. Wasn't he sound in business, a man of his word? Hadn't he given money to most churches in Gorham, and every other worthy cause?

And as for Negroes, it didn't come up. For as far as Gorham knew, there weren't any. Apparently no one suspected, and yet it worried Thyra Johnston. One night she said to her husband,

"Daddy, what are we going to do when the children grow up?"

"Maybe we won't have to do anything. Let's just saw wood and see what happens."

Their colored friends down in Boston knew the Johnstons were "passing" for white in Gorham but they were used to this and did nothing to hurt them, although some of them didn't like the idea, called them not only "passing" but "on the other side," and would snub them. But these, Thyra Johnston points out, were "mostly those who were too dark to 'pass' themselves. Yet even of these dark ones, some understood why we did it, and said they would do the same if they could."

Frequently the Johnstons made trips to Boston where they visited with old Negro friends, but on these they never took their children who had seldom heard the word "Negro." And, if they could not invite these Boston Negro friends to visit them in Gorham, most of them understood.

Gradually they were growing into the town. The popular new doctor was presently elected to the school board, as well as to the Rotary Club and the Masonic Lodge. Thyra Johnston became active in civic work and also in bridge clubs, and with the little parties and teas which make up the life of every small town. Twice she was asked to take the presidency of the Gorham Women's Club, and was elected president of the White Mountain Junior League of the Congregational Church.

But in their little rented house they were crowded, the children were growing, and why shouldn't they buy a house of their own? At first they had been fearful because who knew that the colored thing might not slip out, and then where would they be? Better to be able to leave on a month's notice. But as they made real friends—ones who might not care much, even if it did get out—they felt more secure.

As for houses there were several, but the one their hearts were set on was the recently vacated "house on the hill."

"Oh, Daddy," said Thyra Johnston, "wouldn't it be wonderful if we could live up there?" It was

three stories with seventeen elm-shaded rooms looking down on all Gorham, with a large reception hall
and two parlors.

"Well, why not?" said the doctor. And so they did.
And gladly they lent its yard for the Christmas tree
of the Congregational Church, and the house for its
Christmas social. All of Gorham came. The church
ladies made more money that year than ever they
had before. It was just as crowded for their New
Year's reception, and soon it easily was the gayest
and most popular house in town.

But that summer there was an incident which
frightened them, and yet somewhat reassured them.
Thyra Johnston's father (no one would dream he
was not all white) had come up from Boston for
a visit and one afternoon the entire family went
swimming. Loitering on the bank while the others
splashed, her father fell into conversation with a
man whose name he never knew and whose face
he could not remember.

"See that lady down there?" asked the stranger.
"Well, they say she's a real mulattress. But now,
funny thing is, her husband's darker'n what she is."

"You must be very much mistaken," said Thyra's
father, "because that lady is my daughter."

The Johnstons now knew that people must have

been talking. But since the father reported the stranger had not said it in a hateful way, only as something curious and interesting, they hoped it might not make too much difference if it did get out.

The family had been living up on the hill three years when they went to Boston for a year. Dr. Johnston had been offered a position as a Roentgenologist at a nearby hospital if he could get the training. He realized that it was time for him to develop a medical specialty, so he applied and was admitted to a post-graduate course in this specialty at the Harvard Medical School—the first Negro, so far as he knows, ever to study Roentgenology there.

But moving the family to Boston was a problem, for there was the matter of the children.

"What if we run into old friends?" asked the doctor.

Thyra Johnston pointed out that "our colored contacts are mostly weaned away now. No one knows but Mother, and she won't tell. And, if I run into any of them on the street when I have the children, well, I can handle that."

For that year they took a tiny apartment in Brookline, and little Albert, who was now eleven, went to a public school, and here first ran into that race prejudice which is common in most large cities. There was a fairly high percentage of Jews there and, because he was darker than most, he was immediately asked, "Are you a kike?"

He wasn't, but one of his friends there was Bob Abrams, whose father was Rabbi of the Beacon Street synagogue. It could happen to anyone who was dark. It was like the time back in Gorham when in teasing their French-Canadian maid, he had called her a "Frenchman," and she had spiritedly retorted by calling him a "little picaninny." His mother had become unaccountably angry and forbade either of them to use such language again. But why was it so important? The maid hadn't really minded when he had called her a "Frenchman."

He liked Gorham much better than Brookline, and was glad when the year was over and he could go back to high school there. He quickly made the honor roll and although at first he was not good at skiing, he managed to take second place in one of the slalom races. He was doing remarkably well in piano, too, and that was the year when he played as his little brother sang "Bless This House" at the Congregational Church Children's Day Service, and it so moved the people that they not only cried, but when it was over they clapped right out in church.

Their minister, who had been a graduate of Mount Hermon School in the Connecticut River Valley of western Massachusetts, recommended this school strongly for Albert. And it happened that, just as the application came through, a splendid opening developed for his father at the Keene hospital, a direct result of his X-ray work at Harvard. It was a struggle to leave, because the family was now so securely settled in the little town below the hill, and Dr. Johnston so well known that even the dogs didn't bark when he came to the door. But it was a step up in his profession which he could not fail to take.

In Keene some of the Congregational ladies called early. But it was not as it had been in Gorham. "It was probably me, being supersensitive," confesses Thyra Johnston. Still more probably it was because Keene was a larger and therefore colder town, lacking the village intimacy. It takes any stranger at least a decade to become established in New England. However this was, the Johnstons again got conscious of the "colored thing." Even had it come out in Gorham it might not, at the end of their stay there, have mattered too much. But here, among strangers!

And things were not too smooth for Albert at nearby Mount Hermon. His first roommate was an

Irish boy (he did not stay long) who cared only for
athletics and horses and the Irish.

"Some people think I'm Jewish, but I hate the
Jews," he told Albert. He was always proudly flexing
his muscles, and looking curiously at Albert's olive
skin.

"What *are* you?" he was constantly asking. "A
kike or a Greek or what? No? Well, I bet you've got
some nigger in you." And then he would be off, talking proudly about his muscles. But this didn't bother
Albert, although now and then he wondered how a
little German blood could make such a difference.

After the Johnston family had lived three years
in Keene they felt secure enough to buy the big
house they had been renting on one of Keene's best
residential streets. But meanwhile the doctor, who
had been following the papers closely, realized war
was coming. Long before Pearl Harbor there were
appeals to doctors to join up, and finally a special
meeting of New England doctors was called in
Boston. War looked probable, they were told. Since
they would have to go anyway, "the earlier you get
in, the better commissions you will get." There
was the further fact that Dr. Johnston was deeply
moved by the war and anxious to help if his country got in. And twice the Navy had approached him
with offers of a commission.

"There's no question about my being qualified," he explained to his wife. After all, wasn't he a Diplomate of the American Board of Radiology, as well as a member of the A.M.A.? Of course, had he been known as a Negro he might not have attained either, but this had not come out. "If the Navy does accept me," he went on, "people can say what they like about us, but we will have given our children a real background!"

Yet everyone knew that candidates for all commissions were thoroughly investigated, and this he feared. "It's not an ordinary investigation," he would say, in moments of doubt. "I'd be exposed all around."

But, deciding to chance it, he went down to Boston for his physical, and came back greatly elated.

"There's no question, I'm accepted," he told his wife. "And now we won't need ever tell the children anything." The Navy had been most anxious to have him, they explained, as in the whole country there were only 2,200 radiologists, and many of these were over-age or essential.

When a neat young man knocked at the door shortly after this, Mrs. Johnston was out shopping. And when the neat young man told the maid he was not a patient but still wanted to see the doctor, the maid asked him to sit down. When the doctor came in, the young man rose very politely and said:

"Dr. Johnston, I am sent here by the Bureau of Naval Intelligence to ask you a few questions." Then he looked down at a paper. "You graduated from the University of Chicago in 1924?"

"Yes," said the doctor.

"We understand that, even though you are registered as white, you have colored blood in your veins."

"Who knows what blood any of us has in his veins?" said the doctor.

The neat young man, who had been asked to sit down, now got up. "Thank you very much, Doctor," he said. "That is all we want to know." And he left. He had been very polite.

That evening Thyra Johnston tried to be helpful. "Maybe they will still take you. Maybe they only wanted to be sure what you look like—that you aren't really black."

But it was useless, for a few days later the letter came from the Bureau of Personnel in Washington saying that it was "unable to approve your application because of your inability to meet physical requirements."

Meanwhile it was getting embarrassing with his

friends and with other doctors, many of whom were not eager to go into uniform.

"What's the matter with you, Johnston—why are you still around? Thought you were so anxious to get in this thing."

What could he say?

But if the Navy and the "white" Army would not have him, Thyra Johnston urged, then why not the "colored" Army? Several Negro divisions were being trained to fight in Europe. Surely they could use a Negro specialist. If the whites did not want him, better to go frankly and openly with his own people, regardless of rank, than not to go at all.

So he took the matter up through colored channels, clear up to Judge William Hastie in the War Department, telling them the whole story, including the fact that it was not known in Keene that he was colored.

There were some weeks of hope, and then finally a letter arrived in which his supposedly powerful Negro friends admitted that it was hopeless. And on that evening little Albert returned from Mount Hermon with his praise for Charlie Duncan, the Negro who had offered to give up his place in the skiing meet.

III

Breakdown

NOW up to the moment that Albert Johnston, Jr., that evening, had turned off the hot water in the tub and raised up to hear what his father had to say, he had in his thinking been a normal New England boy, with most of his life before him during which he could, like any other New England boy, eat and sleep where he chose if he could afford it, ask any girl he liked for a date, plan any career which pleased him and follow it to the limit of his ability.

Of course he had told his father he was proud to be colored, and his father had delightedly shaken his hand.

And he *was* proud, only what exactly did being colored mean? Naturally he would not hurt his father's career by telling anyone. But suppose he did tell people? How many of those things could he still do? In just what places could he eat or spend a night, how many of the girls he knew could he call for a date, and what would they say if they knew?

Of course they didn't know, and mustn't know, on account of his father. But suppose, for a minute, that they did—then how many restaurants would let a Negro eat in them, and how many girls would just as soon be seen dating a colored boy, and what kind of job could a colored boy get after finishing college—if a colored boy could get into a college?

But why worry about this? Because he hadn't changed, had he? He had been doing all these things before they told him, so why not keep right on? What was different? Nobody was supposed to know, so why should it matter?

Only suppose they did know. Oh, well, skip it.

Yet when he got back to school he found you couldn't skip it. Here he was, a senior now, and in the choir, the glee club, assistant editor of the senior yearbook, and captain of the ski team. But what would happen if everybody knew? Maybe not much. But you couldn't be sure. He quit having dates at the seminary as the other boys did. He didn't exactly decide not to, but every time he thought of calling a girl, then he thought, suppose she knew? Or found out later? If he could tell them, at least he would know the answer, which might not be so bad either way. But there was Dad and he couldn't.

The previous fall he had made the honor roll at Mount Hermon. He was still sixteenth in senior class by midyear, but now his marks were beginning to slip.

Sure, you were supposed to study. But for what? Suppose you worked hard toward some job when you got out, and then they found out? What kind of jobs could Negroes hold? Maybe he was studying all the wrong things. Presently he had the medical department worried with a curious rash. They gave him shots for it, and when it didn't clear up, someone said it might be a nervous rash.

But in the spring they had a seminar on American and foreign relations, and for this Albert really worked. He got from the library a lot of data on the American Negro—not only statistics, but the conclusions which sociologists had drawn from them. He organized them well and presented them eloquently. So much so, that they asked, without suspecting, "Why are *you* so interested in this?"

He had been working in the Admissions Department and became obsessed with the suspicion that perhaps there might be discrimination against Negroes even at Mount Hermon. Charlie Duncan had been admitted, but was there a quota? They said no, but he persisted. If he found as many as twenty or thirty Negro boys who were really qualified, would all of them be let in?

All, insisted the Admissions Department, and for a while he felt better. But, as he remembers it, "I got out of Mount Hermon in an awful state."

Although his first choice of colleges had been Dartmouth, he also applied to Williams and went there for a personal interview where he was rejected because, they explained, his marks weren't high enough. It was true these had dropped since mid-year, yet they were still above college entrance requirements; but his father's reaction was, "They have looked you up."

Which was true? Maybe they didn't have to look him up—perhaps the interview had spoiled it. There was the French-Canadian maid who long ago in Gorham had said, "You little picaninny!" And then his first-year Mount Hermon roommate who had asked persistently:

"What *are* you, anyway? I bet you've got *some* nigger in you."

The remarks had seemed so unimportant. But were they? Now that he knew he was colored, he

began looking for Negroid characteristics in others
—even strangers.

"Gee, he could be colored. He certainly has the
hair for it." Or maybe it was a flat nose, strong white
teeth, or an unusual jaw. There was also Negroid
speech inflection which occasionally would slip out
of someone seemingly white.

In the middle of this came a letter from Dartmouth accepting him, and he thought his troubles
were over.

But in Dartmouth he seemed to be out of everything. He had never felt that way before in any
other place or school. His roommate was a St. Paul
boy whose friends all had a lot more money than
Albert, and spent it like water. Even tuition was
$450 and, with his father just getting on his feet
after the move to Keene, Albert, who earned his
spending money waiting tables, couldn't afford to sit
in on any of their poker games. Also they were all
looking ahead to the war, training for commissions,
and leaving for the Army or Navy every day. But
what did this mean for Albert? If his father had
been unable to get a commission, how could he
hope?

He was, he remembers, in a terrible state of mind,
and began to get queer notions. He would go up on

top of a high tower (it was, he felt, the only place he could study) and then become afraid he would jump off. His marks dropped, because what was the sense in anything? Something in the back of his head, something he couldn't quite think about, had to get settled. But he didn't know what it was so he couldn't get it settled, and then came the feeling that he wanted to die.

At this point his father came up to Dartmouth and took him out of college (the dean promised to hold his place open) and from there to Dr. Solomon Fuller, a well-known Negro psychiatrist who had been born in Liberia, and whose wife, Meta Warwick, was an even better-known sculptress. They had been old friends of his mother's family in Boston. "We felt," says Thyra Johnston, "that we could tell Dr. Fuller everything."

Dr. Fuller talked to all of them and of course particularly to Albert, asking why he wanted to die (Albert didn't know) and how he felt about being a Negro (of course Albert had been proud). Then Dr. Fuller said there was nothing wrong with Albert which time could not cure, but that he was to be allowed to find what he wanted to do for himself, and that his parents were not to push him.

The trouble was he could think of nothing he

wanted. For three weeks he worked in the Boston post office as a clerk and carrier, but it was "too simple" so he dropped it and came home.

Finally he decided to try the Navy. His father warned him he would never get by the front door, but he passed the exam as a hospital apprentice, second class, and went to Rhode Island for three weeks' boot training, during which they were given all kinds of tests. Albert's marks on these were unusually high so they called him in to ask if he would like to take radio training—his speed reaction had been outstanding—but he refused this. For suppose they sent him to some naval base in the South, or suppose it meant a further investigation of his past; what would happen?

So now he was given hospital duty for medical corps training, and this he remembers as the most boring part of all.

Nothing to do all day but scrub decks and think. So many things he didn't want to think about, but now he couldn't help it. The more he thought the harder it was to see any way out for him. He got more depressed, more jittery, wanted to die. Finally, one night in December, he remembers, "The whole bottom seemed to fall out of my stomach, and I began shaking, not knowing what I was afraid of.

But I was smart enough to know this had something to do with my nervous setup, so I ran to the hospital.

"There they sent me to a young lieutenant who was a psychiatrist. I told him I had had this reaction before, but had lied to the admitting psychiatrist because I had wanted to get in the Navy, although I knew I wasn't perfectly stable."

They notified his parents, wrote to Dr. Fuller for data, and immediately sent him to Hospital Pavilion 13, which, Albert explains, "was the nut house."

"For five days they would allow me no razors, knives, or forks. The first night I was confined by myself, observed on the hour. Then they let me out in the ward with the other patients. The man opposite had dementia praecox—with complete loss of mind. Another tried suicide by strangling, but only mangled his throat and looked horrible next day. There was a colored epileptic who would throw fits, and another man who spent all his time reading the Bible. Then there was a schizophrenic who painted what he called modernistic pictures, and so far as I could see, he was right about them.

"Finally they brought me out for tests, and I helped them in every way I could, telling them everything except about that colored business. They gave me the ink blot test among others and said it showed I had a huge imagination, but that this was a good thing, not a bad one. They said my co-operation was excellent. Then they asked me how I would like to leave the Navy, and I told them that I thought I would. Actually I was overjoyed.

"So I was discharged as a psychoneurotic unclassified, but it took three weeks for the papers to come through, and I had to spend these in the hospital. Often we would argue politics, and I guess I would usually bring up the Negro question.

"I remember one day we argued as to whether or not communism would be a good thing for the American Negro, and in the heat of the argument I came right out, told them I had Negro blood, and used my father as an example of what happened to Negroes in America.

"But most of them wouldn't reason. In talking about the Negro I would say he should have social equality as well. But their feeling for the Negro stopped when he had three meals a day. That was as far as they would go, and some of them said I would be strung up for such thoughts. Others said, 'Hell, we're all nuts here anyway, and what we say doesn't mean anything.' "

✦

His mother, after he got home, was also worried about his point of view because, as she explains, "I just call that rabble-rousing."

His father was even more gloomy. He had had high hopes for this son who now seemed not to care what he did or what happened to him. They finally persuaded the boy to take a job in an ink factory in Keene but, as Albert explains, "I got nervous and let a pot boil over," and after they called the fire department he quit, and wouldn't come back, even though they asked him to.

Because, what purpose was there to anything until the bigger things, the ones he couldn't talk about, got straight in his mind?

To his father, it seemed as though the boy was content to mope all day around the house. Sometimes he would play the phonograph. There was an album of "Songs of Russia" recorded by the famous Negro baritone Paul Robeson, which he would play over and over. And his father, seeing the moping, would explode to the boy's mother,

"If you saw as many nervous people as I do, you wouldn't want to come home to another!"

But there was more than that, because, as he explains, "My whole reason for existence had been to produce children who would contribute something to life. Of them all, Albert had been the most brilliant and the most perceiving. Now he seemed too weak to stand up to life, as his mother and I had done—seemed a total loss to us and to the world. So what had been the use of it?"

So it also seemed when the boy turned from the Paul Robeson records to the piano, which he had hardly touched for three years. His hands idling over the keys, he would play all day long and sometimes far into the night, and again he would often repeat one phrase over and over.

He was trying to write something of his own.

"There was nothing to it," he now explains, "— that is, musically, it had no coherence. It was sweet and very sad. But it was my first." A little tune which started brightly, but somehow got overwhelmed with sorrow and wandered off into plaintive dissonant chords, a tune which could find no ending. A song of hopelessness which didn't seem important, except that it was the first thing he ever wrote down.

By now his father, who was very angry at the way things were drifting, decided something should be done. This was a matter for real treatment in a veterans' hospital and after much writing around, he got the necessary papers drawn up and ready for signing.

But when Albert's mother understood that this was really a commitment, she was furious. She said the family should stick by the boy, not put him in the hands of others. And after putting up what Albert now describes as a "terrific stink," she finally got the whole thing cancelled.

Yet, what could a family do for him? The melancholy moods continued. "I was scared of people, and I didn't know why," says Albert. "I wandered from this to that and there was constant friction with my father, who wanted me to go to school and make something of myself." But what was the point in school?

And now another problem came up. "A lawyer who was indisputably colored was coming to visit us," Mrs. Johnston remembers, "and we decided we couldn't put off any longer telling the other children—that is, Donald, who was then twelve, and Anne, who was a year younger, but not Paul, because he was then only seven."

Donald remembers that he and Anne had been playing out in the yard with about twenty other kids, when she called them in the house. But before they went upstairs to bed, she told them to wait in the living room, as she had something to say.

"Daddy's going to have a guest," she explained, "darker than anyone you've seen, but don't embarrass him with questions. The man is a colored man.

"Also I want to add that you children are colored too—not as colored as he is, but we are all supposed to be colored."

At first Donald didn't believe it, and then he didn't like it.

"What do you mean, I'm colored?" he asked. "Isn't my face as light as yours?"

Afterward when they went upstairs, Donald came into Anne's room. Of course it did explain some things. It explained why all the other kids they knew had seen their relatives or been to visit them while they never had—only Aunt Nette, who was very light, and Mama's folks had ever been to Gorham or Keene. And it explained a lot of whispered talk they had overheard from Mom and Dad about the race business, about how the colored were doing this and that, stuff that Donald had paid no attention to. But still it didn't really make sense.

"Did you ever think we were colored?" he asked Anne.

"No. Does it make much difference?"

"I just can't believe we are. I have the features of

a white person." Then he walked over to her mirror and stood looking frowningly at his blond, curly hair, his light brown eyes, his fair complexion.

He looked at them for a long time.

IV

New World

IN late spring an old friend of Albert's from school days in Gorham named Walt called to say he was hitch-hiking to Syracuse, New York, and invited Albert to go along. So why not?

If you are with an old friend for several days and have something on your mind, it's pretty hard not to tell him, so by the time they got to Syracuse Albert told Walt everything.

"All right, so you're part colored. But what difference does it make? Why are you so worked up about it?"

It was like putting down a huge load which he had carried for more than a year.

The funny thing was that Walt not only didn't give a damn, but wasn't even interested in it. It was almost disappointing.

In Syracuse, they decided to go on to Buffalo and have a look at Niagara, since they were so close. And in Buffalo, Albert said why didn't they keep on going? Because it was fun being out with a guy who knew, and yet wasn't even interested, seeing people who didn't make you worry about what they thought, or how they might react if they really knew. It was fun just drifting along and seeing the country. Albert began to feel much better.

So why couldn't they go on—maybe to Cleveland —he had an Uncle Melbourne who lived there.

Walt said all right, let's. Maybe this uncle could put them up or at least get them jobs.

Then Albert said probably he could, but there was one thing, Uncle Melbourne lived in the Negro section.

Walt said, gosh, that would be fun, they could live down there and it should be interesting and different.

And this to Albert was just as though someone had socked him on the head and jarred something loose. Of course it would be interesting, and far more to him than to Walt. Because here he was, colored himself, and he didn't know anything about colored people or how they thought and lived, except for Mom and Dad who didn't count because they lived just like everybody else in Gorham or Keene. But if you were colored, well, certainly you ought to know about it—if things were different, just how were they different, and if it was bad, just how bad was it?

Suddenly he wondered if he hadn't been curious all along, only scared to find out. Well, he wasn't scared now, because Walt wasn't scared, just curious. And Uncle Melbourne, his father's own brother, would understand and treat them right.

Which he did. Uncle Melbourne was a bartender in a wealthy Cleveland club. Walt got a job as a steel-burner, and Albert a job with Chase Brass and Copper Company. After work they would go to night clubs in Cleveland's Harlem. "We had a great time," says Albert. "Lots of them were good, some of them were low, but it was all interesting." And here for the first time he met a colored girl who fascinated him—it was just a flash, yet it was the first.

But presently they were restless, particularly Albert. Uncle Melbourne was good to them, but he was a bachelor. In the back of his head Albert kept wondering what Negroes were like in their homes —you couldn't find this out in night clubs.

Well, he had other relatives in Chicago and still more out on the Coast. So when he said to Walt, why didn't they start out and really see America, Walt thought it was a swell idea.

In Chicago he knew Cousin Ben Prescott lived in

the Rosenwald Apartments. They went through fifty blocks without seeing a white face. Walt didn't care —he was getting a big kick out of it. Again this cousin introduced them to his friends, and again there was a very pretty colored girl, Lauranita Taylor, who fascinated Albert. He was still more pleased to find that there were plenty of colored girls who were just as much fun to know as the girls in Gorham and Keene. And maybe that had been one of the worst parts of finding out about this colored business—wondering how all the girls he had known or ever would meet, would react if they found it out.

Well, there was nothing for these girls to find out—nothing to be afraid of—and they were just as much fun as the others. It was a big thing to know and he wanted to know more, not only about this colored business but about the whole country. Chicago was big and interesting, but the whole West was beyond it. And New Hampshire, even New England, began to look small.

Walt wanted to see it too. When they left Chicago, hitch-hiking west, Albert had $5.00 in his pocket which they figured maybe would see them through to the Coast and, if not, something would turn up. Just out of Chicago cops stopped them right and left looking for draft dodgers, but they had their discharge papers.

It began to get rough in Iowa, where it was very hot and progress was slow. Nebraska was hotter than Iowa had been, dry with a scorching wind. The country as far as you could see was flat, like walking along on the bottom of a dry ocean. The elm trees since they left New England had been getting skinnier and skinnier until now in the little towns they were almost saplings.

One night they hopped a Union Pacific freight going west, and found that their car was loaded with huge concrete pipe sections about seven feet long. They had no idea whether they were headed for Denver or Cheyenne, but hoped Denver because they had heard the Cheyenne cops were rough as hell.

Sometime between midnight and dawn the train must have stopped, because they were wakened by a lot of bouncing thuds and crunching noises—a big crane was lifting those seven-foot pipe sections out of the car, so they crawled out of theirs and ran like hell, right into the middle of Denver's Mexican district.

They didn't know any Spanish but they both managed to order coffee. Walt had a hamburger and Albert tried a bowl of chili and it was good and filling. Back of them were the hot flat treeless plains, stretching away like an ocean of sod and sand. Ahead they could see the sharp high black outline of the mountains, rising up 14,000 feet above the sea. It was quite a country.

They hitched automobile rides for three hundred miles west of Denver, but at a mountain town called Tobanasha, a fellow at the station told Albert that the desert was on the other side of those big mountains, so they decided not to risk thumbing rides but to hop a train. They didn't know much about deserts, but they decided they'd better stock up. They spent almost all of the dollar and a half they had buying peanut butter, saltines, and canned orange juice. That seemed about right for a desert. They then hopped a train headed for Salt Lake. First it went through some beautiful mountain formations— twisted rocks they had never seen before—sliding around big canyons like a snake. As they gained altitude it got a lot colder. Pretty soon the freight pulled onto a siding. They were both thirsty and since they wanted water they started off toward a little creek they could see. But while they were down on their faces drinking, the train started, and by the time they saw it moving it had picked up quite a bit of speed. They made a dash for it, stumbling across a swamp, but the rotting grass and mush sucked at their ankles and they missed it, and now they stood there wondering how they would spend the night. It was bitter cold. Walt had some dry matches in his shirt pocket, and they were about to build a fire when they spotted a little shack on ahead, just off the right of way.

Inside was a curious old fellow who reminded them of some hermit in a story—sitting there in a litter of egg shells, beer bottles, and broken glass. The place had no lights or water, but the old fellow made them welcome, cooked a dozen eggs for them in a rusty skillet over his fireplace, and then offered them bread and beer. They ate all of this and thanked him. Then he put some food in their knapsacks, saying they might need it tomorrow, and they thanked him again.

He then told them to lie down and get some sleep, that a westbound freight was due through about three-thirty in the morning which would be going slow here on account of the grade, and he would wake them when he heard it.

For a while Albert lay awake listening to the wind whishing softly through the pines, and the fireplace embers popping now and then as they died away,

and smelling the pine needles and the smoke from
the fireplace, and now and then raising up to look at
the outlines of the big rocks. Gee, it was a big country, and yet, if you were in trouble, there were
people who helped you and didn't ask any questions.
A country so big there ought to be room for everyone to get along.

Lots of it was nice, and none of it was as bad as
you could imagine if you didn't know it. And another
thing—far away out there in the darkness at the end
of this railroad track was Los Angeles where his aunt
and uncle lived in the colored section. There he
could really find out about this colored business in a
way that wouldn't touch him so closely as if it were
at home in New England. After all, if it got too hard
to take, he could always slide out of it, because he
had never seen any of these people, and need never
see them again.

But why not stay long enough really to know
what living with Negroes was like—get all those
questions answered which he could feel in the back
of his head? And now that he could feel them as
sensible questions instead of fears of things unknown, his head was feeling a lot better.

The next he remembers, the old hermit was shaking them awake. In the black dark, a long pencil of

bluish light was stabbing up the hill, and they could hear the double-Diesel chugging up the grade. They ran for it and piled aboard, into a car full of steel slabs which were icy cold after the warm floor of that shack. Six hours later they were out in the baking desert, those slabs so hot you couldn't touch them. All they had to eat was dry sandwiches and that peanut butter on those dry salty crackers.

At dawn the next morning they read a sign on a station which told them they were out of Utah and grinding past Caliente, Nevada. They hadn't been able to rest much because of the jarring and grind-ing—they had had no real sleep for a week. And at Las Vegas, Nevada, they were caught in the act. The deputy sheriff was a tough baby, gave them a dress-ing down, and told them they couldn't hang around, but were to hit the highway quick for California.

They went into town for coffee and a hamburger, but again were afraid to hitch auto rides through this desert country, so they walked out to the edge of town and jumped the same freight, which was loaded with defense equipment. The next morning, when it stopped for awhile at a little border town just over the California line, they hopped off for a look around and to stretch their legs. This part of California wasn't so different from Utah and Nevada, just more of those hot blue mountains covered with sage and buckbrush, except where it was irrigated in the green valleys. Presently their train rolled into and through some kind of huge arsenal and power plant. There were guards all around, so they crouched low, and here inspectors were put on the train. They decided to hide separately—Walt in a car of coiled barbed wire ticketed for the Marine Barracks at San Diego, and Albert in a car jammed with huge truck wheels, each about five feet high.

But soon the guards also moved, and got so close they could hear them talking. They waited until the train started around a bend skirting a mountain, a curve so sharp that the guards would have had to look through the mountain to see them. Then they climbed out on top and scampered over the tops of about fifteen freight cars to a safer place. They were so tired they both dropped into a doze, and were awakened by the guards shaking them. It was four o'clock in the afternoon and the train had stopped at San Bernardino.

Now this was a defense train and they were afraid the guards might turn them in as spies or saboteurs. But they were good guys who only said, "Sorry, you fellows will have to get off here."

All that afternoon and night they sat by the high-

way, trying to thumb a ride to Los Angeles, but
didn't get one until seven the next morning, when a
friendly truck driver picked them up and at eight-
thirty dumped them off in the middle of Los
Angeles's Mexican district.

They were starved, their clothes dirty and almost
in rags, and Albert didn't want to look up his aunt
and uncle in this shape. So they found a sign "Money
to Loan" and Albert got $12 for his wristwatch. With
this they bought a pair of pants each and some sox.
Then they went to a lunch counter and each ate a
half-dozen eggs with bacon and toast, and drank
three glasses of milk and a cup of coffee.

"It all tasted swell," Albert remembers, "and now
I felt in shape to get in touch with my Los Angeles
relatives, foremost among whom was my Uncle Fred
and his wife. He was extremely light, and had married a woman somewhat darker than he. I also knew
they had a son, and that they lived on the west side
near the 'Sugar Hill section' of the Negro district,
so called from Sugar Hill in Harlem where the well-
to-do Negroes live.

"I got a big surprise. It was a large district with
fine palm trees, well-trimmed and watered lawns,
three-story houses as nice as any I had seen. When
you ring the doorbell a colored maid usually answers.

The district was beautifully laid out and somehow reassuring to me.

"In this district live Negro doctors, lawyers, engineers, and merchants. Most of them make their money, not from the whites, but from other Negroes. The merchants own one or more stores—sometimes a little chain—where they serve Negro customers and also employ Negro help, which most white-owned chain stores will not do.

"I first met my aunt, whom I had never seen. But when I asked for my uncle, I found that much had happened. He had owned a business and had been fairly well-to-do. Also, he had been interested in politics and had gone as a delegate to a National Convention. This he had greatly enjoyed. But when he got back to Los Angeles he found that his enemies were saying that he wasn't really interested in helping his race, that he was out only for himself and his own advancement, and had become a 'White man's Negro.'

"There may have been other things behind it, but this incident decided him. He divorced his wife, married a white girl, moved to another state, was now 'passing' as white, and had cut himself off completely from all his former Negro friends and from everyone who had ever known that he was colored.

But my aunt, whom he had divorced, although terribly wounded by all this, had never betrayed his secret. Why? I found that no Negro ever does, although they bitterly resent it.

"They will condone a Negro who 'passes' for white only if it is temporary and for the purpose of getting an education or holding a job. But outside of these, they expect them to come home and spend their entire social life with Negroes. This they call 'temporary passing.'

"However, 'permanent passing,' in which a light-colored Negro leaves his race and spends all his time with whites, is another thing. 'It's all right to pass for a job, so long as you socialize with us,' they say.

"My uncle was not only 'passing,' but 'on the other side.' Yet so strong is the tie between all Negroes that, although they bitterly resent a Negro who has 'gone over,' they will nevertheless guard his secret as though it were their own, and not expose him to a white man.

"As soon as I arrived at my aunt's house, she telephoned her former husband to tell him that her nephew had arrived in California. Although he had been extremely fond of me as a child, he refused to see me, but only sent his best wishes. Why? Maybe because he wanted nothing to do with his former wife and their Negro friends. Maybe because he was afraid I might be dark, and so would betray him to his new white friends and white wife.

"I found that he was far from being an isolated case. The number of cross-bred people, many of whom now 'pass' for white, is greatly on the increase. The last census listed 12,800,000 registered Negroes in the United States, but some Negroes believe there may be as many as 13,000,000 additional cross-bred people not officially registered as Negroes, many of whom now 'pass' for white and some of whom do not even know that they are colored.

"In our own family, we can count fifty who are registered as white and who can 'pass.' There are many thousands of colored people, even in the South, who 'pass' as white. Some may be rather dark, and people may be doubtful of them, yet they travel freely on southern Pullmans and busses because the companies are now fearful of making mistakes, since they have been sued by Greeks, Jews, and other dark-skinned people.

"Many light-colored Negro men 'pass,' as my uncle did—you never see them again. I found that the one ambition of my seventeen-year-old cousin was to 'pass.' His mother, who couldn't do it herself, was very much against this. After all, she lost a husband

who went 'on the other side.' This urge to 'pass' is
very strong in light-colored boys. As soon as they
get on their own, many disappear and their families
never hear of them again.

"I also found that light-colored Negroes are often
prejudiced against darker ones, and many will not
associate with someone completely black. The ma-
jority of Negro political leaders are light. People try
to say that this is because they are smarter, because
of their mixed blood. But I know this is wrong. It
is only because, in any difficulty with the whites,
Negroes will send a light-skinned one to negotiate
because they have found it easier for him to ap-
proach the whites.

"In the arts and sciences, however, light-skinned
Negroes certainly do not predominate, and sociologists find just as high a degree of intelligence among
the dark, as they do among the light-colored ones.

"In general, when barriers and boundaries begin
to break down, white people usually prefer light-
skinned Negroes to dark ones. For instance, Lena
Horne, who is light, might be allowed to live in
Hollywood, whereas a man like Rochester, who is
very dark, might not.

"Another interesting thing about prejudice is that
it always increases with the numbers of the minority.

If there are only one or two Negro families in a town, usually there is little or no prejudice. It grows directly in proportion to their numbers. And this is not only true for Negroes, but for almost any minority race or religion. Only where numbers are involved do you have prejudice, and then, the closer you get to marital relations, the stronger they become.

"During my trip across the country I think I learned the exact degree of prejudice in the average white American. They did not know I was colored, and the average man would say, 'Yes, the Negro deserves an opportunity. I know of many intelligent, hard-working Negroes. But we think they must keep their place.'

"But when they come to know Negroes, this prejudice usually fades. For instance, a friend tells me that while she was working in the O.P.A. office, one of the clerks was a girl from South Carolina who threatened to quit if they hired a Negro girl. They did it anyway, and several weeks later the two were going out to lunch together.

"Yet most white people are ashamed of prejudices and often try not to show them. For instance, if I bring a colored boy into a college dormitory room, everybody makes an extra effort to be polite. They will all get up, say, 'I'm very glad to know you,' and ask him to sit down. Whereas if I bring in a strange white boy, they will scarcely look up, say 'Hi' and go on playing the piano or studying. All Negroes who have had much contact with whites are just as accustomed to this 'over-politeness' as they are to open prejudice.

"But back now to Los Angeles. When we arrived at my aunt's house she was overjoyed to see me, also liked Walt very much and asked us both to stay with her. But when I told her that Walt was white, she was embarrassed. She had a very good social position with the Negroes of Los Angeles's Sugar Hill district and she explained to us that, if it were known that she had a white boy staying in her house, she would get a lot of criticism.

"She finally solved it by saying, 'We must present him as part colored and a cousin.'" Walt had no objections to 'passing' in order to avoid race prejudice—in fact he was very much tickled by the whole idea.

"She took us down to a Broadway department store and spent $75 on us for clothes so that we would be presentable to her friends, and then gave a big party for us—inviting the sons and daughters of the leading doctors and lawyers of the Sugar

Hill section. All were good, upstanding, respectable people. They were of all degrees in color—one was as black as that telephone, others were as light as glass curtains, and still others were what Negroes call 'mariny,' which is a definite type in between: golden skin with reddish crinkly hair.

"It was the first large Negro party I had ever attended and it was most interesting. The differences are that Negroes are in general more friendly to strangers than are whites, but their social parties tend to be more formal. For instance, all the girls were primped up in long gowns, and everything was done and served in an impressive manner—much more so than we were used to in New Hampshire. But it was a warm welcome and my father tells me that this prevails among Negroes everywhere.

"The stock questions at a Negro party, after you are asked where you come from, are, 'How do people treat you there?' or 'There aren't many Negroes there, are there?' or 'Are you passing?'

"The rest of the talk was as intelligent as you would hear at any New England party, except that there was of course a lot of emphasis on the racial question. They discussed music and books and colleges—the usual stuff that people of our age talk, but always in terms of Black and White. This I wasn't used to.

"I was asked, 'What college do you go to?' (This is always a very important question.) And when I said Dartmouth, it immediately made me a big wheel.

"Walt was having a wonderful time. He was even more surprised by everything than I was. Some of their questions about the Negro business were hard for him to handle, but he was busy dating up all the better-looking light-colored girls. It was also good for me, as I realized that all along I had been worrying over what they would be like and how they would receive me—fear of the unknown.

"Many things about me fascinated them—the fact that I had been raised entirely among whites and had only recently learned that I was colored, the fact that my father's practice was entirely confined to white people. And they were particularly astounded by the amount of life insurance Dad carried, because they said many companies either refuse altogether to insure Negroes, or will let them carry only small amounts.

"After this party, most of the guests either invited us over or had little parties for us, and soon white people became a rarity in our lives. Yet I had a little trouble. Top Negro society is, as I have said, stiffer and more formal than anything I had been used to in New Hampshire, and my aunt often scolded me for being too exuberant. And in a week or so I began running into their taboos. I would come out with some story of having been to Ciro's, the Macambo, or some other fashionable night club up on Hollywood's Sunset Strip. But then a silence would fall and I could see that they didn't like it. They would say coldly,

" 'We don't go there.'

" 'But,' I would protest, 'you've never been up to Sunset Strip to find out if you can get in or not.'

" 'No, Albert,' my aunt would say firmly, 'we just don't do that out here.'

"My viewpoint was, why should I stop doing things I had done all my life, simply because I had been told I had Negro blood? I had been brought up without taboos—why should I narrow my life now?

"But the Los Angeles Negroes had, for the most part, come originally from the South and had lived as Negroes all their lives. They avoided mingling with whites because they felt they were not wanted and therefore enjoyed themselves more freely in Negro places.

"But there was also a deep pride. For instance I learned of the case of a white woman who had been especially prominent in her world, and who married a Negro professional man who had an equally good position in the other.

"She was bewildered to find that, in spite of all her efforts, it was almost twelve years before her husband's friends would receive her as a social equal.

"Now she understands. They wanted to make sure that it was a really solid marriage, that she had not married him as a stunt or an exhibitionistic thrill, that she was not the kind of mentally twisted person who could only feel comfortable with what she secretly considered her 'inferiors,' and had married a Negro for that reason.

"It took a long time before they were certain, and these were painful years for her.

"It was shortly after I arrived that I met a girl I shall call Helene. I first saw her picture at my aunt's. My aunt said Helene was going to the University of California at Berkeley, was a brilliant student, and very popular in Los Angeles. What I heard of her interested me, and so when my aunt phoned me at a friend's tennis court that she had come to call, I came at once, not even bothering to change out of my shorts. But this didn't matter because she was in slacks.

"We hit it off instantly—it was as though we had known each other in childhood. She was beautiful, a little darker than I was, and had a brilliant mind. She sparkled but had a serious side, too. She wanted to do everything she could to help the cause of the Negro, and all her studies at Berkeley were with this in mind—including public speaking, at which she had worked hard and was very good.

"Her father was dead, and her mother had then married a prominent Negro doctor. They were living in the Sugar Hill section of Los Angeles. Helene had read everything, and she dressed simply and extremely well.

"I was tremendously taken with her and we spent a lot of time together. I would go over to her house, which was big and very beautiful, and she would cook Sunday night supper. She was as fascinated by my story as I was by hers.

"'Al, what's it like to be white?' she would ask. She wanted to know exactly what type of house we lived in, how it felt to mingle with white people, and exactly what my father did. And what had been my relations with white girls? Had I ever kissed them? And I would ask her the same questions, because I knew as little about colored people as she did about whites.

"About this time my interest in music began to come back. My aunt rented a piano. It was mostly for Helene that I felt I wanted to compose something big and important—something that would make her proud of me.

"She was very popular with the boys. Once when I came over there were four there, but she smoothly got rid of them so we could talk. She wanted to know everything—what my ambition was in life, and my reaction to being told I was colored.

"I told her that now for the first time I felt really happy about it. This pleased her. She was darker than I but not too dark, and I told her I thought she could get by if she ever wanted to, although actually there might be some doubt as there also was in my case. She told me a white lieutenant had once taken her home, and later had told her that he had not dreamed she was colored.

"About that time I decided I had been wasting my time, and enrolled in the University of Southern California under the GI Bill of Rights because I wanted to study more music and also journalism. In addition, I went out for skiing, and early in my first term was elected secretary of the ski club.

"We would take trips into the mountains. At the club and at the University I suppose they assumed I was white, although I didn't tell them so. However, I saw no reason why I shouldn't take my colored friends along.

"I asked one of Helene's girl friends and also my cousin to go. The girl, who knew they thought I was white, said 'No, I don't think I should go. I don't want to embarrass you.' However she was broad-minded and did not object to my 'socializing' with whites to this extent.

"But when my aunt found I had taken her boy, she was furious. He was very light, as his father was, and would have no trouble 'passing.' It was in fact his ambition to do so when he grew up.

"My aunt said I was a bad influence, and that I was only a white man's Negro.

"It seemed also that, at the University, some of the Negroes were saying I was snobbish and avoided speaking to them on the campus. This certainly was not true, and their critical sensitiveness annoyed me.

"So I decided to move out of my aunt's house, away from that whole atmosphere which seemed thick with taboos and suspicion, and move into one of the University houses where I could lead the normal student's life which I had always had in New

Hampshire. Walt decided he wouldn't go to school, and presently went back to New Hampshire.

"Helene's girl friend also understood, but she warned me: 'You're going to have trouble with Helene. She's been raised differently from you.'

"I was sure she was wrong, and the night I moved out of my aunt's house I took Helene to a movie and afterwards told her what I planned to do, and why I wanted to do it. That it wasn't desertion—it was only keeping one's freedom and not arbitrarily narrowing one's self to a small group.

"She listened quietly that evening. I suppose I did all the talking. At last she said, 'Well, go ahead if you want to.' And that was all she said. How was I to guess what she felt?

"At the University, my roommate—a white boy of course—was studying for a degree in international law because his father had found gold and lead on a big ranch they owned just over the border in the Mexican state of Sonora. We got along well, but were both busy. I was intensely interested in music and could hardly wait for the weekend to call Helene.

"But it seemed she was busy. Her voice over the phone was friendly, but the old warmth was gone, although I couldn't admit it to myself. Also I noticed that some Negro students, as we passed on the campus, were deliberately avoiding my eye and cutting me when I spoke. For them there were two worlds. If I had anything to do with the other, I could not be part of theirs. And I had crossed some kind of boundary.

"There never had been boundaries for me, and I felt that there should never be. But when I would go back to my aunt's it wasn't the same. She had been very fond of me before. Now she was nice to me as a visitor.

"Well, even if my own people had become aloof there was no reason why I should isolate myself, so I started going out with white girls although I really cared for nobody but Helene. But it wasn't a success. I found I had little in common with them, and also began wondering how they would react if they knew I was colored. Maybe I should tell them and find out. But then the old fear came back—I was unsure of myself again.

"And about this time I went to the hospital for an operation. It was not a serious one, but I had to stay there ten days. My aunt knew of it, yet neither called nor came to see me. Nor did Helene. Maybe they had cut me off. Maybe they considered me as 'on the other side,' and felt if they visited me it would betray me to my white friends. In either case the result was the same.

"The whole thing had failed, and as soon as I was out of the hospital I packed my trunk and went home."

V

Release?

IMMEDIATELY after Albert arrived in Keene there was more friction with his father when Albert said he wasn't ready to go back to school. His father said he had no ambition. Albert feels that this wasn't quite true. He was thinking a lot about Helene, and his music was coming more and more. His time at the piano wasn't just mooning, although he had no real knowledge of harmony.

But he didn't know yet just what he wanted to do about college, so he got a job soda-jerking at the Howard Johnson restaurant just at the edge of Keene. In the evenings he would go out with the girls of his old crowd. But this now bothered him, just as it had with the white girls back in California —what would happen if they knew? There was one he particularly liked, and finally after he had gone with her for a few weeks, he decided to tell her. But she interrupted him to say that all of their bunch of girls had already heard it whispered about, and so had talked it over among themselves, and it hadn't seemed very important to any of them.

But this wasn't always the case, for Albert Johnston points out that, even in tolerant New England, intolerance rises when marital relations are involved. There was a second girl who also had already known it, but who one day said to him, "When I came out with you today I got in a little squabble with my boy friend," and explained that she was going with Albert "only on a friendly basis, and that was as far as it should go."

And there was another family in Keene, with a daughter only a little younger than Albert, who said that "While of course Albert is one of the finest boys who has ever come to our house, still . . ."

Yet things were getting straighter for him now and he decided to enroll in the University of New Hampshire. Its music department was particularly good, and he felt he had gone as far as he could on his own without knowing something of the theory of harmony.

Meanwhile, Albert's younger brother and sister had been telling him their problems. Donald, after he was told, clearly was unhappy about it, so his parents took him down to Washington—"so he could see other light-colored people," explains his mother.

"And he liked them very much. But he doesn't want to mix the two races." And when Anne says anything about their being colored, he will say, "Not so loud!" When colored relatives come to visit them in Keene, he doesn't ask his friends over to the house while they are there. But when he is with all Negroes, he isn't embarrassed, except with the darker ones.

As for Anne, her parents and Albert are glad to say that she "is proud of it," and so she is. "The boy I go steady with," Anne explains, "told me it didn't make any difference. And my high-school friends never say anything to embarrass me."

"Of course," Anne adds, "now and then there is a slip. If someone is passing around a pack of cigarettes and they accidentally miss someone, that person may say, before he thinks, 'What's the matter, am I colored?' Then there is a silence."

The Johnstons know another colored family who live in a small town in a nearby New England state, and who have a daughter a few years older than Anne. This girl is about to enter college but, although she is a skilled pianist, she refuses to study music there because, as she explains it, she would "wind up pounding the keys in some café, which would not represent our race properly."

People in her town have always gone out of their

way to be nice to her and, in spite of the fact that she is dark brown in color, she was elected an officer in her high-school class.

As a child she played with the children of the very best families in that town where her family has lived for twenty years. She went to every high-school party until this, her senior year, which is the time when most girls develop serious beaux. Then she began to drop out. Since there are no colored boys in that high-school class, there was no one to bring her. But as Dr. Johnston, who knows human nature well, points out, "She might have been similarly ostracized among Negroes who were light and close to 'passing.'"

Anne is not quite at this age. At sixteen she is very pretty, with large brown eyes, a soft olive skin, and soft brown curly hair. Not long ago her parents took her down to Tuskegee Institute where her mother's sister is assistant purchasing agent for the school. Her husband, George Reed, teaches engineering on the Tuskegee faculty. Anne had a wonderful time with the colored people there.

There was Lieutenant Elliot Grey, who took her up in his plane, and taught her to drive his convertible. Everybody on the street said hello and then, having seen her with Lieutenant Grey and learned her name, would call her up for dates without being introduced, which seldom happens in New England. Tuskegee was one friendly family. She also met Eugene Dibble, Jr., son of a well-known Negro doctor, as well as Timothy Tilden who last year was in Amherst, which is not far from Keene, and who invited her down in November. She took Shirley Keating with her from Keene, and Timothy got Shirley a blind date with the white boy he roomed with. Then Timothy invited Anne down for the Amherst formal on May 9, and her father let her take the snappy convertible with the red leather cushions, and six other boys and girls from Keene.

Eugene also visited them one weekend in Keene, and Anne had a big party for him, inviting all her high-school friends.

Both Anne and her brother Donald are very popular in Keene high school. Donald plays hockey, is manager of the football team, and is in the band and the dramatic club. Anne was elected both cheerleader and vice president of her class. But sometimes she is uncomfortable. It's all right in Keene, where everybody knows her. "But at each game," as Anne explains it to Albert, "I have to meet cheerleaders from other towns, and I don't know how they will react."

It isn't easy.

"And another thing," Anne adds, "it would be different if we were either black or white. But this in-between stuff!"

And there was that recent discussion she had with three other kids. It started with a southern lynching which was in that day's paper. Anne had said how awful it must be. One of the boys in the discussion was the high-school valedictorian, and with them were another boy and girl—all good friends of Anne's.

Well, the valedictorian had said, of course Negroes are okay, but keep them in their place.

When Anne argued, he agreed that some were intelligent, but that most of them were just cotton pickers. Then he asked her if she would marry a darky and she said sure, if she wanted to. And wouldn't he?

And he said no. Even though Lena Horne is good-looking, he wouldn't marry her or any of them, because it would be so awful bringing up children and not knowing what color they would be.

Then all three of these good friends had turned on Anne, asking her who she was going to marry. And she answered, someone like herself.

"What do you mean by that?"

"Just someone like myself," Anne insisted. But not very happily. Because it isn't easy.

Donald also enjoyed the trip down South, although on a good many things he doesn't agree with Anne or with Albert. Of course it was different inside Tuskegee. He had a wonderful time with them, too, and it amused him to hear them jokingly call each other "spooks." The whole thing, he says, was a real educational experience. But after you get outside those gates, he doesn't like it a bit. There was that outdoor movie with the big sign "Colored People Not Allowed." He went in anyway, yet he felt uncomfortable. But his first experience with race barriers in the South was one day when he hopped out of the car to buy an ice-cream cone at a dairy bar. People were queued up in two lines, and a colored girl was filling the cones.

Without particularly noticing, Donald walked over to the end of one of the lines, and was waiting his turn when he felt a tap on his shoulder. He turned around and there was a cop.

"Son," said the cop. "Over there in the other line."

"Why?"

"We got laws down here," said the cop. Donald looked and saw that the cop was pointing to the white line, and that he had been standing in the

colored one. The cop had assumed he was white.
But Donald can't see what difference it made. After
all, wasn't the same colored girl going to give him
his ice cream anyway, no matter what line he was in?

And then last year, back home, something happened. There was a girl Donald liked who was the
daughter of a prominent Yankee family and the
children had always played together ever since she
and Donald were in the sixth grade. But one day
he got a letter from her, a very nice one except that
she said she had hoped to see more of him, but that
it would be impossible because she was forbidden
to do so.

Of course a thing like that from someone you are
fond of would bother anyone, but Donald presently
was able to find out that it wasn't anything he had
said or done, it was the girl's father. He was an old-
fashioned Yankee and it wasn't only Donald, he felt
the same way about Catholics and Jews—just wanted
his daughter to stick to the English. Only the funny
thing is, he doesn't object if his daughter sees Donald's sister Anne. They are very fond of Anne, and
Donald thought they had liked him, too.

It's all pretty confusing and a nuisance, hard to
figure out what you should do or how you should
feel, and sometimes Donald and Anne have argu-

ments about it. She asks him who he is going to marry and he says, "Anyone who comes along—Chinese, I don't care."

But Anne says she's willing to bet her life she would never marry a white person. And Donald thinks this attitude is all wrong. "Anne's been listening to the colored people at Tuskegee until I think she's anti-white," he says, defiantly. He thinks, although he says the others won't agree with him, that learning about it has made a difference to everybody in the family. And each has reacted to it in a different way. His way is that you shouldn't make any big point of it, that it shouldn't make any real difference, and that you have a right to act the way you really feel, as he is doing.

And what of Dr. Johnston today? Well, that Navy incident has left its scar. "Before," he remembers, "I was always a good mixer." He still smiles and says hello on the street, but he has resigned from the Rotary and quit going to the Masonic Lodge. "I guess I've become morose," he says sadly. And then, apparently apropos of nothing, he tells his story of the white piano. It concerns a woman who taught music and who, as a girl, always dreamed of owning a real concert grand, white and with gold legs. Then, after many years, it all came true. But by then, it was just another piano, and in spite of its gold legs it didn't sound anything like the white and gold piano in her dream.

Since the Navy incident there has been no difference in the attitude at the hospital, but somehow he doesn't try to make outside friends any more, is content to "sit down, make a living, and that's all."

And why? Well, what else is there to do? Back in 1944 he was offered an association with the head Radiologist of Wayne University, the largest medical school in Detroit. But he felt he would have to refuse. There are occasional race riots in Detroit, and the doctor feels that if he went he would have to "pass" completely, with the always present danger that he might suddenly be out of everything.

Then there is the other side. There was serious talk of an offer from a large Negro college in the South. But should he make his family conform to social conditions of the Deep South? "And me too," says the doctor. "It would take me five years to learn how to live down there."

As for the country generally, so far as the Negro is concerned, the doctor feels that in recent years there has been not an advance but a regression. It could never have been worse than it is now, but it has become worse in the North, for Negroes are now barred from a few places even in Boston, where in his day this was unheard of. In general he feels there is more prejudice in America, although it is not legalized, than there was twenty-five years ago, although in the fields of art, literature, and sports it is much better, and among actors, painters, musicians, and writers the Negro finds almost no prejudice.

But away from home where he is unknown, Dr. Johnston finds a good deal of it. At medical conventions, southern doctors will tell him earnestly, "Johnston, you just don't know the problem. Negroes don't have the brains, or any sense of moral values like you and I have. You have to treat 'em like that."

He would like to come out openly as a Negro, but had he done so, could he have achieved what he did? Only the trouble now is that, in spite of his own accomplishment and everything he has done for his family, "Whatever I do, my race gets no credit." And, thinking of this, he presently says, softly, "I have more or less an empty life. Maybe a little like the white piano with the gold legs."

How do New Englanders feel about the Johnstons now that a number of people have learned the secret? Well, although the Johnstons didn't know it, there have been rumors for years. "Do you think it's true they are colored?" people would ask each other. Only in New Hampshire it didn't greatly matter what the answer was, for it was not considered very important.

And somehow New England feels that it shows its tolerance by not emphasizing it one way or another. It isn't polite to be too interested in it, or to mention it before the Johnstons. As one of the doctors who works at the hospital puts it, "Johnston has never told me, so why should I tell him?"

Why should not the children play with the others and have a normal social life in the high school? Why shouldn't the Johnstons live in one of the nicest houses on Keene's best residential street? New Hampshire sees no reason.

Then there is Gorham, a much smaller town, where the Johnstons are more intimately known even than in Keene, and where, the Johnstons thought, their secret was even more carefully guarded. But was it?

Mrs. Ensign Barrett, wife of the druggist, remembers the day the Johnstons first came, when she saw her husband getting out of his car and walking across their lawn with "this little stranger, so very dark." And she said to herself, "Who in the world has Ensign brought home now?" But then Gorham got to know the little stranger better, and soon he was no longer a stranger but a country doctor who would come at whatever hour of the night you called, and brought friendliness into the room when he came. And Ensign enjoyed him so much at the store—there were those nip-and-tuck checker games between the druggist's prescriptions and the doctor's calls. And they liked the children, too: little Albert, always so bright and talented in his music, and little Anne, "such a dear little thing."

As for the dreadful secret which the doctor feared might wreck his career, the matter of his race wasn't exactly "discussed." That is, it would never be brought up officially in any large gathering like the White Mountain Ladies Circle. But from the very first it was "generally mentioned." Something was different about the Johnstons, and Mrs. Barrett remembers talking it over with the Libby girls as to what they might be—colored or Indian or maybe Jamaica Negro. In the end they decided it was better to "live and let live" because, as Mrs. Barrett said at the time, "Whatever Dr. Johnston is, he's a very nice man."

And that is the verdict of New England.

As for Albert, who is now at the University of New Hampshire, when he first came he was imme-

diately asked to join a Greek letter fraternity. But
he thanked them and said no. Suppose he joined,
and this colored thing came out, and then some of
them didn't want him? Would it be fair to them?
And would it be any fun for him?

But the thing which influenced him most was
meeting Bill Ballard in connection with one of
those seminar discussions on domestic and international problems. This one had touched on the
Negro question and Bill Ballard, one of the few
Negroes at the University and a fine, level-headed
boy like Charlie Duncan, had stood up and given
the Negro point of view.

Albert Johnston had said nothing then, but afterward he had come to Bill Ballard to say that he had
particularly enjoyed it because he also was colored.
Bill had looked at him sharply, said he never would
have dreamed it but that he was glad Albert had
told him, and of course he would tell no one if
Albert didn't want him to.

But then they had a long talk on this last point.
And Albert finally said, "Well, after all, why not tell
everybody? Why carry a lie around all your life?
And if you really want to help the Negro, isn't the
first step to stand up and say, 'Sure, I'm one, this is
the way it is, this is how it feels to be colored.'

And then if you amount to anything in life, if you can make something beautiful, isn't the Negro race entitled to credit for it? And aren't you cheating your own people if you deny them?"

Bill warned him that it wasn't going to solve the race problem. Color lines would still be here for many more decades. "But," said Bill, a little sadly, "it might help blur them a little around the edges, and that would do something for all of us. Boundaries wouldn't be quite so sharp."

Just as clearly as Albert remembers that time in their house in Keene, when his father, standing in the bathroom door, told him, "Well, you're colored," he also remembers that college seminar. Of course, some of his close friends had been told it as a secret. Probably most of his other friends had either heard or guessed it. Maybe a good many other people who did not know or like him very well already suspected it.

But a good many people suspecting something is far different from everybody knowing it as a fact forever, and this is why Albert Johnston remembers even the room the seminar was held in—a medium-sized college lounge with about twenty students sitting a little listlessly on the upholstered chairs.

After Bill Ballard had finished his part of the discussion of the Negro problem and sat down, and it was time for him to rise, Albert remembers thinking that, even now, he didn't have to go through with it. Because if he did, it could never be undone. All his life he would sit, pencil in hand, before those printed blanks which read "Race: White or Negro ——" and for him there could be only one answer, if he went through with it now.

It was nice to know he could still draw back, even as he was rising to walk up to the platform. He need only leave out a few sentences of his prepared talk, making it a general discussion of the Negro problem, and then later explain to Bill, who would so easily understand, that he had realized he was too young to make so final a decision, that he should first get more firmly established in his profession and in life, before taking so crucial a step.

This is why he remembers that the first row of chairs was empty, but those back of it fairly well filled; remembers which of the girls looking up at him from that second row were cute, and which were not; remembers how at first, the twenty listened listlessly until he came to the place where he said he felt that perhaps he could contribute something to this discussion of the race problem by telling of the problem of crossbred peoples, because he was himself a Negro. And of course he remembers how, at this point, there was a rustle as that crowd of twenty leaned forward to look, first at him, and then to glance at each other. He remembers how very still it got then—as it gets at the climax of a concerto. And then, just as in a concerto, that feeling of great release at the end of a struggle.

And what difference has it made?

At the University of New Hampshire, very little that he can see. His friends are still his friends, he makes new ones about as fast as the other boys do, and now it seems like a lot of pother about nothing.

Only he feels better himself. There aren't any more secrets, nothing to be afraid of. And he can go ahead writing his concerto based on that tune he was going to lay at Helene's feet, a concerto which the music department says shows a real grasp of harmonics and deep feeling. No longer a heartbroken little tune which can find no ending, but a slow, sad, sturdy song for all his people.